THE WEALTHY CREW MEMBER

Simple steps you can take to save, invest, and plan for retirement while working behind the scenes.

BY

ANDRÉ RAMIREZ

www.TheWealthyCrewMember.com

Printed in the United States of America
ISBN-13: 978-1492233954
ISBN-10: 1492233951

Disclaimer

This publication is designed to provide accurate and authoritative information in regard to the subject matter covered. This publication is sold with the understanding that the author and publisher are not engaged in rendering legal or financial advice or other professional advice, and they assume no legal responsibility for the completeness or accuracy of the contents of this book. The author and publisher specifically disclaim any responsibility for liability, loss, or risk that is incurred as a consequence, direct or indirect of the use and application of any of the contents of this book. If expert advice is needed, the services of a competent professional should be sought.

This book is dedicated to you... the people of the Industry. You work hard to help other people make a lot of money; now it's time that we focus on your wealth.

ACKNOWLEDGEMENTS

I would not be here if it weren't for the love and support of my family and friends. Even if you weren't directly contributing to this book, please know that you did in your own way. Thank you all for all the support over the years no matter what crazy thing I was trying. Thanks to my father Lupe Ramirez for teaching me the value of a hard day's work, and to my mother Marji Ramirez for all the support over the years.

I wish to thank all the financial experts that have had an influence on my life, and who have helped me to learn the habits of managing money. A special thanks to T.Harv Eker who helped me get to the root of my bad money habits; Robert Kiyosaki whose book *Rich Dad Poor Dad* enabled me to buy three investment properties before I was 29 years old. To Hector Riviera who introduced me to the man-Napoleon Hill and forever change the way I thought about money.

I am very grateful to Anaita Bahadurji for her continued support and all her hard work editing and formatting this book. This project would not have been completed without you.

Thanks to Eve McCarney who put up with my ongoing changes, and who worked well below her rate to design an amazing cover.

Thanks to the L.A. fambam – Brandy Card and Joe Papiernik, Bob and Erin Stillman, Brian and Emika Scotti, and Paul Helling for all the support over the years.

Finally, thanks to all the amazing people I have worked with in this industry.

Hello...I'm Hollywood.

No, not the Hollywood that you see on T.V. or in the movies. No, I'm the Hollywood that makes things happen. The Hollywood who rushes, hustles, and loses sleep. The Hollywood that is there before everyone setting up, and the one that is there after everyone has left. The Hollywood that plans, builds, and executes. The Hollywood that nobody recognizes on the street. The Hollywood that misses family time, and the Hollywood that still has bills to pay.

Yes...I'm Hollywood.

WHY SHOULD I READ THIS BOOK?

Have you ever had any of the following thoughts?

I wish I had more money to spend.
I have to work or I can't pay my bills.
This show doesn't pay enough.
I want to take time off, but I have to work.

On November 5, 2007 the writer's guild decide to go on strike, and within a few months of that, the Screen Actors Guild would have a dispute which created a work stoppage. Add an economic crisis due to the collapse of the subprime loans market to this, and it was not a good year for members of the industry. Do you remember where you were during this time and what show you were working on? Most likely you were affected or knew someone who was. The writer's strike and the shortage of work had a dire effect on the people of the industry. People lost homes, and couldn't pay their bills. The union emergency funds were emptied in order to help people, and it seemed as though the industry had shut down. Although this was a while ago, it doesn't mean that it can't or won't happen again.

Let me ask you a couple of questions…

- *If another strike was to happen, or let's say that you got hurt, or for some reason you couldn't work in this industry any longer, how long could you survive financially?*

- *How long before you started to lose everything that you have worked hard for?*

This is an industry where inconsistency of work is the norm. Some months are great while some are slow. You often hear the saying feast or famine. As crew members in the Motion Picture Industry we have seen tremendous change in the last decade with regards to pay. It seems as if there is a new contract or side letter for every job we start. There are tiered rates, and shows with special concessions for vacation and holiday pay. Contracts where weekly rates can be turned into daily rates when it is convenient, and a host of other negotiations that have been made on our behalf. Although you have little power in the negotiations, where your power lies is in your money management.

What about when it comes to retirement? Will you have enough to maintain your current lifestyle during retirement? Do you even know how much you will need in order to retire? Are you concerned that you will not have enough to retire, and that you will be forced to work long after your retirement age… eventually killing over on some cold sound stage; the crew pausing momentarily and the AD yelling out, "That's a hard five" as they come to get your cold lifeless body? Well, whether you have or not, let me tell you what this book in your hand can do for you.
In this book you will learn:

1. How you can manage the money you have.

2. How you can budget for the inconsistence of work.

3. How to change your bad money habits into good ones.

4. How to learn to control money and not have it control you.

5. A way to never fight over money with your spouse again.

6. How to figure out how much you need to save for retirement.

To be absolutely honest with you, all the information contained in this book is readily available from top financial experts. This is not a book with get rich quick formulas. The book in your hands will give you, the hard working crew member, the tools you need to better manage your money. What I have done here is gathered all the up to date financial information and created a simple guide for you to follow. Whatever knowledge I possess I am gladly sharing for the betterment of my fellow crew members. I pass along the truths that help me to manage my money. I once was very broke, and struggled with debt. I am still on the road to reaching my financial goals, but the knowledge that helped me to get on the road to wealth is written down in these pages. Read this book carefully, discuss it with other people, and debate it whenever you can, for the lessons in this book, if applied properly will help you to achieve your financial goals.

Here's to your financial journey!

-André

If you don't want to read the whole book, here is a summary: Track your expenses, monitor your income, make sure one is higher than the other, and save for your retirement. To find out how and to gain some financial intelligence … read on.

CONTENTS

DEVELOP YOUR MONEY MINDSET

Your mind is the key to your financial success. It is through your past experiences that you make your current financial decisions. In order to successfully manage your money, you must understand the belief systems that have been programmed into your mind. Understanding the psychology of money will help to lead you to future wealth.

UNDERSTAND YOUR HABITS AND CREATE GOALS IN ORDER TO ACHIEVE THE DESIRED OUTCOME

When you begin to understand your habits and start to create financial goals, you begin your journey to a stable financial future. Take control by being aware of your habits and determining your goals.

DEVELOP A CLEAR UNDERSTANDING OF WHERE YOU ARE FINANCIALLY

The beginning is everything. It is from here you can measure your success. With a thorough understanding of where you currently are financially, you can begin to formulate a plan for the future. Understanding your current financial position and setting goals for the future will prepare you to make great strides towards becoming a wealthy crew member.

IMPLEMENT A SYSTEM

It is through a system of money management that will align you on your path to great wealth. Like the North Star to a sailor, implementing a system keeps you on track and allows you to reach your financial destination. The F.I.L.M. system will be your North Star along this journey, and the M.A.D. F.I.T system will be your destination.

KEEP A PORTION OF EVERYTHING YOU MAKE

Your ability to continually and consistently keep a certain percentage for yourself every time you are paid, will lead you to a financially safe future. Do not wait until the time is right to pay yourself. It is through the habit of paying yourself that makes the wealth.

CONTROL YOUR SPENDING

The false idol of consuming leads us to believe that we need more and better possessions. The way you spend will determine if wealth is in your future. This reaction of constant consumption will eventually work against you. Slay the need to justify purchases and make logical not emotional purchases.

Let your money work for you! It is not only important that you keep a portion of what you make, but that you also invest that portion. Allow your money the option to compound and make you more money whenever possible. It is important to create a mindset that your money is a willing servant to help you.

The trouble with managing money can often be traced to the inability of the individual to keep focused on their finances. By having a system that is fully automated, the system of wealth is allowed to happen without interference. Allow automation to lead you to becoming a wealthy crew member.

In order to enjoy things in the future you must plan for them now. Do not be fooled into thinking that things will just work out. It is through conscious decisions made with your money that you will be able to live the life that you desire when you retire.

- INTRODUCTION -

THE F.I.L.M. SYSTEM

Throughout this book we are going to implement the **F.I.L.M. system**. This is an easy way to guide you through understanding and taking care of your finances.

The **F.I.L.M. system** stands for ...

F	*F-igure out what your expenses are.*
I	*I-mplement a system.*
L	*L-everage your money.*
M	*M-anage your wealth.*

*Before we get started I want you to picture
A tiger making a cake while watching sprinklers water grass.*

*Remembering this scene will help to guide you on the path
to managing your money and creating wealth.*

PART I

TIGER

A tiger has an extremely aware mindset; he is methodical in his habits and has strict goals of getting what he wants every day. He has a clear understanding of where he is and what he needs to do.

DEVELOP YOUR MONEY MIND

*Y*our mind is the key to your financial success. It is through your past experiences that you make your current financial decisions. In order to successfully manage your money, you must understand the belief systems that have been programmed into your mind. Understanding the psychology of money will help lead you to future wealth.

FADE IN
INT: YOUR MIND

P.A.: "Why does the Gaffer make the actors smell that white ball before we shoot?"

UNDERSTANDING

THE PSYCHOLOGY OF MONEY

A friend of mine once told me a story about a very new production assistant asking someone on set why the gaffer made the actors smell the white ball right before every scene. What the P.A. perceived to see was her reality. Of course this was not what was happening. The gaffer was merely checking the light levels with his light meter.

When it comes to managing your money your perceptions and reality must match. What I mean when I say this is that too many of us only have an idea of what is going on with us financially, and we perceive what we need. You may say, I just need a better show, or to work more hours. However in reality, you may just need to cut down your expenses and manage what you have a little better.

To further this point, imagine if you took a group of Extras who lived sitting chained to chairs staring at a blank 10' x 16' set wall. (I know you art department people want to decorate it, but for now let's leave it blank.) Behind the row of sitting Extras, there is a 12k light shining on them and crew members are constantly walking between the light and the back of the Extras. As the crew walks through the light, all the Extras can see are the shadows of the crew members that are thrown on the wall that they are staring at. If the extras remained chained there for a long period of time, eventually the shadows of the crew members would become the Extra's reality.

MEANING

When you as a crew member learn to manage your money, it is like a chained Extra who is freed from staring at a set wall. Once freed, the Extra can see the true reality that surrounds them. By you gaining a financial understanding, your perceptions of money will be in alignment with what reality is. Proper understanding is one of the first steps to becoming a wealthy crew member. If you have ever found yourself saying, "I need to get a better show," or "I need a higher rate," then you are not addressing the other end of the question, which is…where is my money going and why? It is as if you are staring at the shadows of the crew members.

There is a secret psychology of money. Most people don't know about it. That's why most people never become financially successful. A lack of money is not the problem; it is merely a symptom of what's going on inside of you.

-T. Harv Eker

EXPLANATION

The study of Neuroeconomics is the combination of psychology, economics, and neuroscience. This field studies why and how people make financial decisions. It is a curious thing that we don't always make decisions that make sense financially, but rather the majority of the time our financial decisions are made emotionally. This means that when it comes to money, how our brains have been wired affects the financial decision over the most logical one.

When crew members have money problems they tend to "band-aid" the problem. They make a temporary adjustment to fix whatever financial mess they are in, but they never fix the core problem. Everything in life is cause and effect. In order to manage your money properly you must look at the underlying cause of your financial challenges. You may not be aware of your core problems, instead only focusing on superficial causes to your money problems such as "I need to make more money." To get to your core money problems we need to find out your feelings about money and align them with proper money management thoughts.

In order to find out your money programming we must understand your influences. Suppose when you were a kid a girl with freckles continuously pushed you, and knocked you down on the playground. Although you grow up and forget about the incident, your brain files this experience. As a grown up there is just something about girls with freckles you just don't like. Even though you don't realize it, as an adult when you encounter a person with freckles your brain pulls up the "freckle file" and sees that a girl with freckles once caused you pain. The brain uses this experience to form a belief that you carry into adulthood.

The same concept of the "freckle file" is used when it comes to memories of money. You can read this book and a thousand others, but they are not going to be of any use unless you understand your core feelings about money. Your relationship with money and your beliefs about money come from the way your neurons have been wired during your formative years. Experiences are your truth, and there is no wrong or right, just your feelings based on your past experiences. However, when those beliefs translate into bad money management, then we need to address them.

One of the most important steps in managing your money is to understand your feelings towards money. An incident, or the way your parents handled and spoke about money has a great influence on your current financial situation. If you take a moment to think about it, there will be a certain memory, image, or saying that you remember from you childhood. This will usually dictate how you currently feel and handle money as an adult.

It will be through examining this memory that you will be able to recognize your current money habits.

ACTION

THE FOUR-FOUR MONEY PSYCHOLOGY

Just like the actors that we all work with have scripts that guide them through their workday, we all have inner money scripts that we have memorized when it comes to money. Just as a movie's success depends on a great script, if your inner scripts about money are positive, then you will be financially successful.

I want you to take a minute and remember four key phrases that you heard about money when you were growing up. Such things as hearing your parents say, "Rich people are terrible," or "We can't afford that," or my particular favorite, "We are going to end up in the poor house." I heard this one constantly from my mother growing up. Imagine a house in which everyone who was poor would have to live together. After you have examined your first memory of money, write down four negative money phrases that you have heard.

After you have your four phrases, I want you to counter those phrases with positive ones. For example, if you wrote "money is evil," I want you to then write the opposite. "Money is good" and three more statements for a total of four. Just like you need exercise to make your body stronger, you need to exercise your money thinking. Here you are doing 4 sets of 4. It is important that as you write the "good money thought" you say it aloud; this combination of writing down the new thoughts, and saying them helps to reprogram the thought process.

Time to do work! Write down negative and positive money feelings.

Here is an example ...

Negative Money Thought	Positive Money Thought
Money is evil.	1. Money is good. 2. Money helps people. 3. Money allows me to eat. 4. Money is a tool to use, just like I use a hammer.
Money doesn't grow on trees.	1. Money can be easily attained. (Legally of course!) 2. Money can easily turn into more money. 3. I have found a lot of money in my life. 4. There is an abundance of money in my life.
Money isn't everything.	1. Money helps me provide for my family. 2. Money funds research to fund diseases. 3. Money allows me to do what I want. 4. It is my job to secure money to help others.
When I die, I can't take the money with me.	1. Money I leave behind will help my family. 2. I save enough money so I can live the life I desire. 3. Money keeps my family safe. 4. Money is the key to a more secure life.

As we continue on your money management journey, we start to reprogram your feelings about money. This exercise should be repeated at least once a month, until your answers are all aligned with positive money association.

INTERESTING FACT

In a research paper titled, The Symbolic Power of Money by Xinyue Zhou, Kathleen D. Vohs, and Roy F. Baumeister, a connection is made with money used as a stimulant to help with social acceptance, and managing pain. According to the research paper published in The Journal Psychological Science, a group of volunteers were asked to count money, and another group was asked to count pieces of paper. Both groups then had their hands dunked in hot water. The volunteers that had been counting the money reported less pain than those who counted plain pieces of paper.

SUMMARY

You're past experiences have a big influence on how you deal with money. It is important to be aware of how your past is affecting your current money situation, and to take methodical steps to change it.

 What To Do ...

1. Open your thoughts to the fact that your reality may be misaligned.

2. Write down your first memory of money.

3. Turn four negative money phrases into positive one.

RESOURCES

Secrets of a Millionaire Mind by T. Harv Eker is one of my favorite books on the subject of the psychology of money. If you get a chance attend one of his seminars, it will be life changing.

"You see, the film studio... is really the palace of the sixteenth century. There one sees what Shakespeare saw: the absolute power of the tyrant, the courtiers, the flatterers, the jesters, the cunningly ambitious intriguers. There are fantastically beautiful women, there are incompetent favorites. There are great men who are suddenly disgraced. There is the most insane extravagance and unexpected parsimony over a few pence. There is enormous splendour which is a sham; and also horrible squalor hidden behind the scenery. There are vast schemes, abandoned because of some caprice. There are secrets which everybody knows and no one speaks of. There are even two or three honest advisers. These are the court fools, who speak the deepest wisdom in puns, lest they should be taken seriously. They grimace, and tear their hair privately, and weep."

- Prater Violet-Christopher Isherwood

UNDERSTAND YOUR HABITS AND CREATE GOALS IN ORDER TO ACHIEVE YOUR DESIRED OUTCOME

*W*hen you begin to understand your habits and start to create financial goals, you begin your journey to a stable financial future. Take control by being aware of your habits and determining your goals.

UNDERSTANDING

One day a craft service person was setting up the after lunch deserts. A teamster had noticed that during the show, the young Craft Service girl would always stack the cookies on the plate in threes, even though there was plenty of room on the platter. The teamster decided to ask the girl "Why do you always stack the cookies in threes?" She replied, "I don't know, the person who trained me always did it." Later in the day, the craft service girl goes on a run and decides to stop by the set of the person who trained her. She poses the question to him as to why he would always stack the cookies in threes. He thought for a minute, and then said, "I don't know, the lady who trained me always did it." He continued, "She is working across the lot, let's go ask her." So they headed over to the set and found the craft service lady who trained him and asked "Why did you always stack the cookies on the plates in threes? The older craft service lady gave a quizzical look, and replied, "Our platters were small."

MEANING

This is a funny story, and a great way to stress why it is important to understand your habits. Do you have some things that you always do a certain way? Have you ever thought about why you do these things? What about your money habits? Here is where we are going to get deep. I don't want this to be like a temporary set that can be put away in a scene dock after we are done. I want to build a strong foundation of money management for you. To do this we have to go back...way back.

Please take a minute and think about your money habits and where they came from. Do you have good money habits or bad ones? Is there a money habit that you need to break? Maybe you buy things when you don't really need them. Or maybe it's impulse buying. Start to track your spending by writing down everything you buy, and see if there are some money habits that you can break.

EXPLANATION

"Watch your thoughts; they become words. Watch your words; they become actions. Watch your actions; they become habit. Watch your habits; they become character. Watch your character; it becomes your destiny."

- A 6ᵗʰ Century Philosopher

Although this quote was written a very long time ago, it is still very relevant. Your money habits determine your life. In the previous section we looked at aligning your thoughts about money and your words through the Four-Four money exercise. If you have not done this please take a moment to do it. The understanding of your habits in the beginning is crucial to help get you on the path to becoming a wealthy crew member. Once your beginning habits are noted, then it is time to write down your goals. If you just wish for things without putting together a strong game plan and without specific things that need to be accomplished, then you are just randomly hoping that you will achieve them. Imagine if a football team knew that they wanted to get to the goal line, but they didn't have strong game plan. There would be just be random throwing of the ball with the hope that a touchdown was made. When an action plan is developed in football or in your financial life, it creates a path to achieve goals. Along the way you will hit milestones, like first downs, that tell you that you are on the right track to your goal. Be realistic in your goals, and set time frames that you can realistically achieve. Remember, you can have both short-term goals and long- term goals.

ACTION

KNOW YOUR HABITS

Please take a minute and think about your money habits and where they came from. Do you have good money habits or bad ones? Is there a money habit that you need to break? Maybe you buy things when you don't really need them. Or maybe it's impulse buying. Start to track your spending by writing down everything you buy, and see if there are some money habits that you can break.

GOALS

In my opinion Google Maps is one of the greatest inventions in the last decade. When I started in this business you would find those big bulky Thomas Guide map books in every crew member's car. If you have been around long enough you will remember the call sheets would list the page number, latitudes and longitude of the location. What were we sailors? Well, that was a long time ago. Now with Google all you have to do is type in the address of the location and you are routed to the destination. Google can also tell you how much time it will take you and if there is traffic. Now, just like Google updates maps consistently, you need to constantly update your financial plan; especially if it is not getting you where you want to be.

Take a moment and think back five years. Where were you financially? Were you better off, worse off, or around the same? There is the old saying that just because a boat is moving doesn't mean that it is going anywhere. This holds true for your money too. You may be making more, but are you continuing in the same spending circles? You must have a destination or in this case a goal that you want to achieve. Without goals things are never achieved. Imagine if the AD didn't plan the day. We would just randomly shoot things, hoping to get the desired result. Don't do this with your money. Have goals and a strategic plan.

What are the goals that you want to achieve in regards to your money? Do you want to be able to take a long vacation once a year? Do you want to have money for your kid's college? Whatever your specific goals are, I want you to take some time and think about your specific goals and write them down. Don't just write I want more money. Instead write, "I want more money so that I can pay my bills." Or, "I want to have $2,400 in savings by the end of the year; I will do this by saving $200 each month to achieve this." The more specific the plan, the more likely you will get that "touch down!"

STOP!

Do not read on before writing down your money related goal.

INTERESTING FACT

Professor in Psychology Dr. Gail Matthews of the Dominican University of California, conducted research on writing down goals and concluded that individuals that wrote down their goals and shared their goals with a friend, were on average 33% more successful in accomplishing their goals than those who just talked about them.

SUMMARY

Take the time to recognize your money habits. Once aware, you will start to notice that certain habits may be hurting your money management.

When you write down your goals you have a constant reminder of what you are aiming for. Listing your goals keeps you on track when it comes to managing your money.

What To Do ...

1. Be aware of your current money habits (break the bad ones).
2. Write down some short term and long term money goals.

RESOURCES

- *The Power of Habit* by Charles Duhigg
- Visit *www.TheWealthyCrewMember.com to* download your *Habits and Goal Worksheet* that will help you track your habits and list your financial goals.

DEVELOP A CLEAR UNDERSTANDING
OF WHERE YOU ARE FINANCIALLY

*T*he beginning is everything. It is from here you can measure your success. With a thorough understanding of where you currently are financially, you can begin to formulate a plan for the future. Understanding your current financial position and setting goals for the future will prepare you to make great strides towards becoming a wealthy crew member.

UNDERSTANDING

"My problem lies in reconciling my gross habits with my net income."

- Errol Flynn

F. | I. | L. | M
Figure Out What Your Expenses Are

YOUR FINANCIAL CALL SHEET

Income/ Assets

The challenge with working in the industry is the inconsistency of earning money. Some months are great and others are not. This is why this book is made specifically for you. There are two approaches that you can take. If you are on a T.V show or a feature or work for the studio and you know that you will be bringing in a certain amount, then you can budget off of that income. If you have been working more sporadically, then I want you to go back over the last three years and see what you have made each year. You can do this by looking at your tax returns or the Social Security office has a record. Take your income over the last three years and divide it by the number of years, in this case 3. This will give you an average per year. Next divide that by 12 to give you an idea of the average monthly income that you make. This will give you a good place to start your money management. The further you go back the more specific. This will be the income number that you can budget to even when you are not working.

Figure out your average monthly income and write it down. (Add up your income for the last three years divide by 3 then divide by 12 = Your Average Income.)

Expenses

The next step is to find out what your monthly expenses are. This includes all your basic necessities and miscellaneous expenses. If you have to pay money towards it then list it! This may be a bit scary, but once you know then we can start to manage. There are two types of expenses that you, as a crew member must track: *Fixed expenses* and your *Variable expenses*.

The fixed expenses are expenses that are around the same every month. This is usually your rent or mortgage, your car payments, utilities, etc.

The variable expenses would be such items as food, clothing, and entertainment. I want you to get a notebook and for the next month write down everything you spend money on and categorize it. When you spend money on gas, a packet of gum, anything over the next month, write it down. Every time you spend write it down. You can also save all your receipts for a month and then categorize and total at the end of the month.

It is important that you write down your expenses over the month, so that you can see where your money is going. **It is best to track expenses for three months to get an average of your variable spending.** For now however, list all your variable expenses and make a guess of what they cost you. This exercise is a real eye opener.

Debt/ Liabilities

Next, let's find out how much debt you are in. You may have read financial books and they may say that there is good debt and bad debt, but if you ask my opinion, it is all bad debt. If you weren't able to get a show and had no income, and couldn't make your payment, how long would it be before you lost your things? That is bad debt. Now take a moment to make a debt column and list all your current debt. This includes any credit card, auto loan payment and mortgages. Let's put this all in a balance sheet.

Here is what your Balance Sheet can look like. On the same sheet of paper list all your income and all your expenses.

Here is an example of a balance sheet ...

Monthly Assets	
Income	$4,800
Monthly Liabilities	
Fixed Expenses	
Mortgage/rent	$1,800
Car	$495
Utilities	$130
Total Fixed Expenses	*$2,425*
Variable Expenses	
Food	$1,500
Entertainment	$400
Total Variable Expenses	*$1,900*
Fixed + Variable	**$4,325**
Debt Liabilities	
House	$530,000
Car	$130,000
Total Debt	*$660,000*

If you want to determine your net worth, simply subtract your liabilities from your assets.

ACTION

Figure out your average monthly income, and then make a list of all your fixed and variable expenses. Finally make a list of your debts.

Do not go on before knowing your fixed expenses and you have an idea of your variable expenses. This book will not help you unless you follow the steps. Now take a minute to write down all your fixed and variable expenses.

Create your balance sheet before you move on.

STOP!
Do not read on before writing down
your fixed and variable expenses!

INTERESTING FACT

If you had 10 billion $1 notes and spent one every second of every day, it would require 317 years for you to go broke.

SUMMARY

What you can measure you can grow. By having a clear and concise awareness of where you currently are financially, you can begin your journey of managing your money successfully. Creating a balance sheet is the perfect way to see your current financial snap shot.

What To Do ...

1. Figure out your average income.

2. Know what your expenses are.

3. Create a balance sheet.

RESOURCES

- Visit *www.TheWealthyCrewMember.com* to download your Balance Sheet Worksheet to track your income and expenses.
- Visit the Social Security website (*www.ssa.gov*) to help find your average income.

PART II

CAKE

In order to properly make a cake you must follow a system. Only portions of each ingredient are put into the cake mix to reach a successful outcome. The process must be controlled and constantly monitored.

IMPLEMENT A SYSTEM

*I*t is through a system of money management that will align you on your path to great wealth. Like the North Star to a sailor, implementing a system keeps you on track and allows you to reach your financial destination. The F.I.L.M. system will be your North Star along this journey, and the M.A.D. F.I.T will be your destination.

SECTION 1

"I used to have a drug problem, now I make enough money."

- ***David Lee Roth***

UNDERSTANDING

EXECUTIVE PRODUCER - YOU

Good producers have a good business sense and tend to be excellent negotiators. They have an understanding of all the workings of the film making process, as well as the financing, distributing and marketing. It is through a close eye on the expenses that a producer is able to stay on budget. Without the skills of the producers, no budgeting would take place. There would be an amount of money and each department would just buy and buy without any restraint. Some may take advantage, (but of course not anyone you or I know.) Most likely what would happen is those fabulous production designers would use up all the money designing the sets before any shooting could get done.

The reality is we are all producers. We are producers of our lives. As producers are extremely important for the production, you are the important one when it comes to the most important production...your financial life. I want you to start thinking of yourself as the producer when it comes to your finances. As the producer you of your life and family, you must have a way of tracking how much money is coming into and leaving your life.

MEANING

If you ask my little sister Natalie, "what is the difference between wealthy people and poor people?" she will tell you, "Poor people talk about ideas, and wealthy people take action." She knows this because I have ingrained this in her since she was a little girl. I have made it my mission for her not to have to go through the years of money struggle that I endured.

This thought of action applies to managing money as well. Wealthy people or anyone in control of their money all have one thing in common- they manage where their money goes. The old saying, "what you measure grows" is especially true when it comes to money. A common misconception or thought that crew members have is that if they had more money then they would be in more financial control. However, this may only be partially true. In the book, *The Millionaire Next Door*, authors Paul J. Stanley and William D. Danko conclude that most millionaires live frugal lives. Their cars are a couple of years old and not flashy, but reliable. They live in modest homes, and they shop for discounts. They have no desire to "keep up with the Jones" but instead save and invest. This core message reveals that true wealth is obtained by how one manages their money. According to Stanley and Danko, one specific fundamental quality that the majority of millionaires have is that their income does not equal wealth. Meaning, that what is important is not how much is made; rather how much of the income is managed. According to their book, these are people just like you who have worked hard, managed their money, and on the outside feel no need to flash their wealth.

EXPLANATION

Any amount of money can be managed. A set dresser that I know only had an extra ten dollars to save after all her expenses. So she began with that, and she learned how to manage her ten dollars. By learning to manage her money, by the time her income increased, she had the tools and practice to properly manage a bigger amount. You see it is not the amount you save; it's the managing of the money you have that that eventually will create the wealth.

It is very important not to buy into the philosophy that you will eventually start saving when you get on a better show, or when you are making more money. This thinking does not work because you won't have developed proper money management. Start today and start with any amount. Start with your next paycheck; it doesn't matter what the amount is, just start managing your money!

F.	I.	L.	M.

Implement a System

Now that you know what your expenses are, it's time to implement a system of tracking your income and your expenses.

Now I want to talk about your money system, and if your money system consists of putting a check in the bank and that dictates what you can or cannot buy, then I would like to invite you to consider changing your system.

Hold on, you're about to have a **MAD FIT**!

34

I have developed two different systems for both single and married people. I will start with the single people; if you are married feel free to jump ahead to the marriage section.

ALL THE SINGLE LADIES, ALL THE SINGLE LADIES (AND MEN)... PUT YOUR ACCOUNTS UP.

Almost every financial book that you read is going to tell you to cut out something from your life, for instance give up spending on your daily latte. Well, I'm not going to do that. There are things that you enjoy in life, and I don't think these need to be sacrificed. What I am going to do is introduce you to a money management system that I call the **Multiple Account Diversification (M.A.D.).** This will make sure that you have money to enjoy the simple pleasures in life, and all your bills are paid. The M.A.D. system is very easy, and by implementing this system I personally was able to save $40,000 in two years (and enjoy my lattes!)

ACTION

Ok, let's get MAD!

The first thing that you want to do is make a list of categories of where your money is going. Below are some category examples. You may have different ones based on your expenses, and that is ok. The great thing about this system is that it's up to you. I don't care where you spend, just as long as you categorize it. Let's take a look at some categories.

1. Basic Needs
2. Savings
3. Investments
4. Savings for new car
5. Fun
6. Vacation

Here you can see that there are six different categories where money needs to go. The basic needs include rent, food and bills. The rest of the categories are self-explanatory. The next thing to do is divide the categories up by percentages. According to most financial advisers you should not spend more than 50% of your income on your basic needs. 20% of your income should go towards your investments, leaving 30% to be broken up into categories. If your basic expenses exceed 50% of your income or you don't have 20% set towards investments, then that is ok. I want you to save and invest what you can. If that means you are only putting in a dollar or 2% in the rest of the categories after your basic needs, then so be it. The goal here is to help you develop a money management system and habit. Eventually you will have the 20% to save.

Here we see the same categories with percentages assigned.

Basic Needs	50%
Investments	20%
Savings	10%
Savings for new car	5%
Fun	5%
Vacation	5%
Donation	5%
Total	100%

Here is how the system works; every time you receive a check take out the assigned percentages and put them into separate accounts. Remember each category has a different bank account assigned to it. You will have an account just for bills, an account for going out, etc. If you are saving for a new car, then open a new account and whenever you have a little bit extra throw that money into your new car account; that way you will have a considerable down payment or you will have months and months of payments saved, so paying the car payment will never be an issue. Remember the goal is to get to the 50%-20% divide, however if you are not there, start where you are. You don't have to do 20%. You can do 1% or 5%. Whatever you feel is comfortable. I repeat **it's not the amount it's the habit.** This is also a great habit to teach your kids, when they get an allowance. Don't put money into one piggy bank; put it into separate piggy banks that are for specific things only.

In looking at the above categories, you will notice that there is a savings and an investment account. The savings account is for emergencies. This is life and unexpected things happen. Cars need transmissions, water pipes break. This account is to make sure that you have some money saved and will be ready for what life throws at you. The investment account is for retirement.

Now that you know how to properly categorize and divide up into percentage, the next step is to open accounts at a bank for each of these categories. (Make sure that they are free accounts.) When you get your paycheck you will divide up the percentage and put it into the appropriate account. Again, do not worry if your percentages are not this high or that you only have 2% for fun. The point of being M.A.D. is the habit. You want a M.A.D. habit!

Once you implement this system you will discover that the great thing about the M.A.D. system is that when you want to go out and have fun or go on a vacation, you can simply look at your account and see if you have enough. You no longer have to have that guilty feeling about spending. That money in the account is specifically for your guilt free spending.

It also helps that when you look into your individual accounts your brain doesn't add up all the accounts. It just associates the current amount in the account that you are looking at. So by default you will be budgeting with a lot less money than you actually have. Now for this to work, you have to stick to the system. If you slip, then get back up and correct it as soon as you can.

Years ago some friends invited me on a weekend trip to Las Vegas. Earlier in the month I went snowboarding so I knew I had used up some fun account money. I checked my "fun" account and it only had $150 left in it. I don't know about you, but $150 in Vegas would only be enough for my Jacuzzi hummer ride to the airport. (Yeah I like to roll big.) So I decided that I wouldn't be able to join my friends even though I had $2,000 in my "Basic Needs" account. This is why the M.A.D. system is perfect. The accounts help to keep you on track, align your spending and most importantly keep you prioritized. Of course you can always borrow some money out of the "Basic Needs" account and repay it later, but what if you didn't work for a while? You don't want to put yourself in a situation where you trade immediate gratification for long term suffering, by not being able to pay your bills. Suppose you did borrow that and you couldn't pay it back, eventually your bills would go to collection, your house would go into foreclosure, and the next thing you know you are homeless. Then you get depressed. You're depressed so you will probably try some heroine to feel better. Now you are a junkie all because you didn't stick to my money management system. Now is this what you want? Ending up on the street turning tricks for a fix? It's up to you.

The difference between this book and a lot of other money books is that I am not going to tell you can't have that or you need to give this up. I want to show you how you can have what you want and still manage your money.

If you start this system and find that you are having trouble staying within a certain budget, I recommend taking out the amount you budgeted in cash and putting it in an envelope. My friend Samantha and her husband kept spending more than their grocery budget. I recommended that Samantha take out the $1,200 dollars that they had budgeted and put the cash in an envelope. This way she could physically see the money dwindling. Guess what happened? Sam came under budget by $200 the month she tried this. She told me that, she just hated seeing the money go.

SECTION II

UNDERSTANDING

> *"There is a way of transferring funds that is even faster than electronic banking. It's called marriage!"*
>
> *-James Holt McGavran*

MARRIAGE AND THE INDUSTRY

Oh marriage, that sacred institution between two people who love each other. Congratulations, you found someone who will put up with your ass... but will they put up with your money management? One of the leading causes of divorce is cheating... but it's not what you think. It's financial infidelity. When one of the partners lies about money it can have devastating effects to the marriage. It is important that each partner is upfront with their money habits. Things like keeping a secret bank account can only lead to fights and your partner not trusting you. Remember if you have a secret bank account and you end up getting a divorce, your spouse is still entitled to half of it. Also make sure that your partner is aware of all your current and past debt.

MEANING

Money problems can cause a lot of distress in relationships. Do you leave the managing of the finances to your significant other, and then when you need money you just take it at will? Just like any good team, everyone on the field needs to know what is going on. It is important that each person is aware of the income and expenses. It will make it easier to achieve your financial goals by having both team members aware of their current financial situation. When one person doesn't know about the finances it eventually becomes a problem.

EXPLANATION

Every couple has their own way of splitting the bills. In the following system you will be shown a way in which equal contributions can be made in order to promote equal amounts of saving and retirement for each individual.

Welcome to the F.I.T. System – Financial Independence Together.

F	*F-inancial*
I	*I-ndependence*
T	*T-ogether*

The FIT system involves contributing percentages of each person's pay in order to maintain a fair contribution to bills as well as to encourage equal personal spending and savings.

In the following example we have Dave and Michelle who both work as crew members. Dave takes home $8,000 a month after taxes from working on features and Michelle is currently working on three camera shows bringing in $4,000 after taxes. Their total household monthly post tax income is $12,000 ($8,000 + $4,000).

At first Dave and Michelle would deposit their checks into their own checking accounts. Michelle would be responsible for paying the mortgage and Dave would be responsible for everything else.

HERE IS WHAT DAVE AND MICHELLE'S SYSTEM LOOKED LIKE BEFORE THEY GOT FIT ...

	Dave	Michelle	Total
Monthly Income	$8,000	$4,000	$12,000
Monthly Bills			
Mortgage	$0	$2,000	
Utilities	$1,200	$0	
Food	$800	$0	
Health	$600	$0	
Car	$200	$0	
Random	$300	$0	
Total Expenses	$3,100	$2,000	$5,100
Individual Leftover Amt.	$4,900	$2,000	$6,900
Individual Leftover %	61%	50%	100%

As you can see Dave has $4,900 left over and Michelle has $2,000 left over. The rest of this money would go into their personal accounts and when Dave or Michelle needs something they just take money out. The problem and maybe you can relate, is that whenever Michelle spends $200 on her hair or Dave spends money on tools or golf clubs, the other would think that the one was spending their money frivolously. This would ultimately lead to an argument. Another issue is that Dave and Michelle were not properly saving for retirement. The F.I.T. system allows for even contributions between both people and more importantly it focuses on putting an equal amount of money away for retirement.

HERE IS WHAT DAVE AND MICHELLE'S FINANCIAL SNAPSHOT LOOKS LIKE AFTER IMPLEMENTING THE SYSTEM ...

	Dave	Michelle	Total Income	% of Income
Monthly Income	$8,000	$4,000	$12,000	
	67%	33%	100%	
Mortgage	$1,333	$667	$2,000	
Utilities	$800	$400	$1,200	
Food	$533	$267	$800	
Health	$400	$200	$600	
Car	$133	$67	$200	
Random	$200	$100	$300	
Total Expenses	**$3,400**	**$1,700**	**$5,100**	**43%**
Remaining	**$4,600**	**$2,300**	**$6,900**	**58%**
Joint Savings	$920	$460	$1,380	12%
Personal Savings	$1,040	$520	$1,560	13%
Personal Checking	$1,040	$520	$1,560	13%
Retirement	$1,600	$800	$2,400	20%
Subtotal	*$4,600*	*$2,300*	*$6,900*	

- Each person contributes 55% of their paychecks towards a **joint checking and savings account** (43% and 12% respectively.)
- 26% goes towards their **personal checking and savings account.**
- 20% is invested in their **individual retirement accounts.**

You can see that Dave brings in 67% of the household total income, while Michelle brings in 33%. If they both were to contribute 43% of their paychecks towards their monthly expenses, Dave would have $4,600 left over and Michelle has $2,300. With the new system after the bills are paid in equal proportions, they both have the same percentage of their income (58%) left over.

Dave and Michelle have implemented the M.A.D. system and created different accounts. (They did not name their accounts, but I suggest adding names to personalize.) 43% of their income is deposited into an account that is just for paying their bills. This leaves them with a remaining 58%. This 58% is then divided up accordingly.

Each person is then able to contribute 58% to the remainder accounts. A joint savings, a personal checking, and a personal savings account with the addition of a retirement account.

With the implementation of these individual accounts, each person has the same percentage of their respective incomes to save and to spend on whatever they like, without the other person getting upset. Everyone is happy!

Marriage
Path to Financial ^ Stability

1.	Each person contributes a fixed percentage towards the expenses determined by the F.I.T. System
2.	Each person puts an equal percentage into their personal savings and their personal checking.
3.	Each person puts an equal percentage into their personal savings and their personal checking.

What if only I work?

If you are married and there is only a single income, it is still important to give the stay at home person their own individual account. Work out a percentage between the two of you, and every month deposit a pre determined percentage into the non-working person's account. This will give them a sense of autonomy and there won't be any fighting when they spend a lot of money on their personal needs.

Can I switch to a different system in downtimes?

The MAD and FIT systems are designed to help you through hard times. You should always stick to these systems even when there are slow periods in the industry. You can however adjust the percentage that you contribute to each account… just keep the habit.

ACTION

Here's how you and your partner can get F.I.T.!

This is a simple math formula. I know…Math. But don't worry it's simple. Try this exercise. Take each of your weekly incomes after taxes and divide by the total amount of your combined income. For example you make $1,200 a week and your partner makes $2,000. This is a total of $3,200 ($1,200 + $2,000). Take the $1,200 and divide it by $3,200 and it will give you a percentage (38%). Then take the $2,000 and divide it by the $3,200 (63%). These percentages are what each person will pay towards the bills. This system is a fair way to split the expenses.

INTERESTING FACT

In 2011 Ohio State University did a study and found that unemployed men have a greater chance of their wives filing for divorce. The same study also found that men have a greater chance of leaving their wives when they are out of work. An interesting finding of the Ohio study was that whether a woman was employed or not, it had no bearing on if the husband would leave. See ladies, we are not all money hungry.

SUMMARY

In order to make a film there is a system. This helps to keep the filmmakers in line with the desired outcome. As you know whenever the system is strayed from, the process breaks down. Make sure that you implement a financial system that is proven to work.

What To Do ...

1. You are in Executive Producer of your life. Start acting that way.

2. Implement the M.A.D F.I.T System

RESOURCES

Visit *www.TheWealthyCrewMember.com* to download your *M.A.D. Worksheet* and your *F.I.T. Worksheet* and get yourself on the road to becoming a wealthy crew member.

"The natives of Hollywood are not the moving picture industry; they merely serve it. They feed it, they clothe it, they house it, and they make it beautiful. The industry itself is a trouper. If is sees a chance for a better stand somewhere else, it will pull up stakes and move forthwith... Hollywood wouldn't be the first town to be developed and then abandoned by industry; nor would it be the first expensive "set" that the film folk have built, used briefly, and then demolished."

–Patterson 1930

- SCENE 5 -

KEEP A PORTION OF EVERYTHING YOU MAKE

*Y*our ability to continually and consistently keep a certain percentage for yourself every time you are paid, will lead you to a financially safe future. Do not wait until the time is right to pay yourself. It is through the habit of paying yourself that makes the wealth.

UNDERSTANDING

"Cocaine is God's way of saying that you're making too much money."

- Robin Williams

We Have Been Pushed Two Months

During the time of the WGA strike I was working at CBS for producers Linda Bloodworth-Thomason and her husband Harry Thomason. When it finally became clear that the production was going to shut down due to the strike, the Thomasons gathered the crew together and said that they were appreciative of our crew, and then said something totally out of character for producers. Harry Thomason told us that if anyone needed money, that they were more than happy to write a check with no obligation to pay it back. It seemed like mere Hollywood speak, but a few hours later one of their assistants came into my office and told me that she was asked to speak with the department heads to reiterate that if someone needed money, they should not be afraid to ask. This was a very touching moment. Rarely does it seem that the above the line cares about our welfare. However, these seasoned producers who had accumulated awards, and were established in Hollywood, were people who didn't just think about their million dollar business coming to a stop, but their concern was about the crew members who worked hard and tirelessly to make their product look good. If you ever have a chance to work for these people, do not pass it up!

Hollywood has a short-term memory. A lot of people lost homes and cars and went into debt because they were not properly prepared for the long down time that the strike brought about.

Just as you put on your seat belt to help you in an emergency, you need to put on a financial seat belt in case of a slow work period.

MEANING

You get up go to work, buy something, go back to work buy something else, go to work and so on. Sound familiar? It is a vicious cycle. As I write this it is a slow period in our business, pilot season has ended, TV shows are on hiatus, and there just aren't that many features going on right now. This happens each year. It seems however, that every time this happens, people are shocked and they become worried. It's like a squirrel that doesn't save nuts. All of a sudden winter has arrived and he is wondering how he is going to survive. You see we know this is going to happen, and sometimes it happens for longer stretches. The amount of time is unpredictable, but the constant is that our industry does have slow periods. My goal is to help you so that you don't have to adjust your life style when we have down times in our industry. This book is to help you prepare for these times. I don't want loss of work to be a case for stress for you and your family. I want you to be at ease and have enough money to sustain you while you figure out a plan b or wait until the work picks up again.

EXPLANATION

Imagine if you had one wardrobe rack, and every day you got 10 coats, and every day you gave 9 of them away, in just 11 days you would have saved more coats than you are receiving every day. (I will give you a minute to think about it. Ok, got it?)

This is the key to being a wealthy crew member. No not selling coats! It's keeping a portion of everything you make. A strange thing that occurs in our industry is that we all make a different amount each year, but we all have the same money challenges. (Lack of it!) Remember that things you need will always grow to meet your income. You must understand that just because you get a show that pays you more, does not mean that you necessarily have to spend more. One of the most important rules to becoming a wealthy crew member is to not confuse what you need with what you want. You have limits to your time so make sure that you place limits on your desires and live below your means.

When it comes to your money it's important to keep a portion of everything you make for yourself. Every finance book and planner lives by this one simple rule: keep a portion of everything you earn. I understand that you have bills and that money could be used to fix the washer, or pay a credit card bill, but you must put money into your savings, or investing account. If you start the MAD system this should be easy to do. Remember, it doesn't matter how much you save, only that you are saving. Start with a small percentage, and then build it up.

When it comes to paying off debt there are different schools of thought on this subject. Some financial advisers say to get rid of debt before saving because when you have debt and are saving it is like filling up a bucket with holes in it.

Other advisers advocate chipping away at the debt while saving. I tend to agree with the latter because the habit your form will be worth more to you than just paying off all your debt.

ACTION

Try this exercise. Pretend that today a strike was called and it is expected to last for 6 months. Write out what your financial and personal life would look like in 6 months from now. How much would you have in your savings account? How would your life and family be affected? After you do that, write out steps you can take to prepare if there was a 6 month strike.

INTERESTING FACT

There is evidence that six thousand years ago in the city of Babylon, the concept of keeping a portion of your pay for yourself was used.

SUMMARY

The Golden Money rule applies in this book and all the other money management books. If you get nothing else from this book, then please take this single rule will help to transform your life. Always make sure that you PAY YOURSELF!

 What To Do ...

1. Write out how your life would be affected if there was a 6 month strike.

2. Write what you are going to do to prepare in case a strike does happen.

3. Develop the habit of using the M.A.D system

RESOURCES

Visit *www.TheWealthyCrewMember.com* to download your *Strike Preparedness Worksheet* and get yourself on the road to becoming a wealthy crew member.

CONTROL YOUR SPENDING

*T*he false idol of consuming leads us to believe that we need more and better possessions. The way you spend will determine if wealth is in your future. This reaction of constant consumption will eventually work against you. Slay the need to justify purchases and make logical not emotional purchases.

UNDERSTANDING

"I would rather carry around a plastic bag with five thousand [dollars} inside, than carry around a Louis Vuitton/ Gucci/ Prada bag with only on hundred {dollars} inside!"

- C. JoyBell C.

If you are the type of person that has to stop by set when you're not working to pick up your check, then you might be living above your means. One of the simplest rules to managing your money is to spend less than you make. I feel that there is this terrible habit in the Film Industry that as soon as we get on a higher paying gig or a long-term show, we immediately start spending more. If you spend more then you are not really making more. Let me repeat that, **if you are spending more, then you are not making more.** This is why it is very important to divide up your check into percentages that you put into your different accounts. This will help prevent you from the "I'm working, I can afford it" syndrome.

SPENDING

The advertising industry is a billion dollar industry designed to make you buy. Consumers have been brainwashed to buy more and more products to help ease their lives, but the reality is that they don't need most of the products they buy. Can you really tell me that, a super blender is really needed? Has blending taking up most of your life, and will the purchase of the blender truly make your life better? You may justify the purchase with the fact of that these products offer convenience.

The problem with that thinking is that the advertisers want you to think you need this convenience. The majority of time they are selling a convenience, it's not one that you currently need. Staying with the blender example, you might not be blending things unless you bought the blender. Do you see how this works?

With the Internet it has become even easier for advertisers to market to your specific tastes and wants. It is a psychological war that you are losing. A big part of controlling your expenses as a crew member is to remember that the key to being a wealthy crew member is to spend less and have more. You have to ask yourself, "Do I really need this?" **Remember, every time you buy something what you are basically doing is trading the time and energy you spend on set to own that thing.** Make sure that each purchase is something that adds real value to your life, and not just something that makes you happy. Also, definitely stop justifying your purchases with, "It's only a day's work," or I can make this up during one show." This is not the attitude of a wealthy crew member.  Make sure that what you are buying is going to contribute to your life in a positive way. Avoid impulse purchases. I use the two-week rule. If I really want something, I wait 2 weeks. If I still want it as much, then I buy it. What usually happens is that I am not as excited and I realize that I didn't really need it in my life. This means I keep more of my money and that means more freedom to not worry about work, or to not have to take a low paying job.

In economics they use the term opportunity cost. This means that whatever opportunity you take, there is a cost for it. If you buy something, the opportunity cost is lack of savings, or having to work more, or not being able to go on vacation. So the next time you want to buy something, remember the opportunity cost.

Websites such as Groupon and Living Social are great sites to find deals, but the problem is that we aren't always looking for a deal. Just because there is a great deal does not mean you have to buy it. It is a strange thing that the human being has, which is the fear of missing out. I am here to tell you, don't worry there will always be a deal if you look hard enough. However no deal is worth your living free and having enough for retirement. Remember that!

DEBT IS EVIL!

The phrase "To pay through the nose" comes from Danes in Ireland, who slit the noses of those who were remiss on paying the Danish poll tax.

Thankfully we don't have a Danish poll tax, but we do get hurt in other ways when we acquire debt. The fallacy in our society is that debt is a good way to leverage your money. This is a terrible misconception. This is what the companies want you to believe. You need to develop the habit of reminding yourself that if you don't have enough cash for it, then you cannot afford it. Whenever you accumulate debt you become enslaved and put yourself at risk. This book is here to give you financial freedom by helping you focus on your needs rather than your desires. The reality in life is that you only need water, food, and shelter to live. All this other stuff is what society and "keeping up with the Joneses" mentality has brought. I am not telling you to move to the woods, but what I am saying is to make conscious decisions when you are going to purchase something. Just like a line producer analyzes every expense to make sure that it is needed for the film.

You as the producer of your life should take on a critical point of view when spending. You don't always need the latest or newest gadget. Think like a Producer! A great experiment to try is not to buy anything for a month, except food and gas.

You will see that you will learn to adjust you life without the things that you thought that you needed.

There are two ways to have more money. Lower your expenses or earn more income. Go through your list of variable expense and see what you can do without. I assure you nothing is more important than being out of debt, not being a slave to your things, and setting yourself up for retirement. I guarantee you the $500 item that you need won't matter a year from now. Don't you think having your money work for you is more important than any immediate satisfaction? I am not saying that you cannot have things. I don't want to advocate cutting out that latte to save money. I am saying that you eventually can have both; you just need to build your accounts slowly to get to the point where you can have both.

Remember, debt keeps you from doing things, and places limits on your life. Repeat this out loud. **Debt is evil!** If you are in debt, then do everything you can to get out. Make getting out of debt a priority. If you have credit card debt, take your highest interest rate and begin paying that account down. Once that is paid down, add the money you were paying and apply it to your next highest interest rate. Continue this until all your debt is paid off. Go back and look at your expenses that you listed and see what you can cut. When you are shopping don't buy the name brand stuff. Use coupons and search for deals. You will be amazed at how fast you can cut down your debt by making a few sacrifices. If you have a family, then get the kids together and explain that you have a goal as a family to eliminate your debt. Write your amount of debt on a piece of paper in large numbers, and put it up in the house. Make a game of it, each month watching the number get smaller and smaller. This can be a great lesson for the kids. Too often parents shield their children from the finances, and instead just preach about how the kids should manage their money.

IS MY HOUSE AN ASSET?

I believe that the biggest myth that our financial system feeds us is the misconception that you own your home and it is an asset. This is completely wrong, and I don't want you to forget this. Your home is a liability; an asset is something that has value and you can make money off of. A liability on the other hand continually costs you money. Let me ask you this question. If you stopped working, how long would it be before you would lose your house? If you tell me that it's paid for, then you have an asset.

Here is the biggest problem with our banking system. You

can pay on your house and get it 99% paid off, but if you stop making payments the bank will take that house right back from you, and will not return the money you put into it over the last 29 years. Your mortgage doesn't guarantee that you will own your home. You are just guaranteed each month that if you make a payment, you can stay.

As a freelance worker you depend on a certainty that this industry will be there for you and that you will be able to continue to make your payments on your house, eventually owning it. That's the idea; but then people refinance and take money out to pay for other debt or remodel, and it becomes harder and harder to pay off your mortgage.

What I am advocating is buying a house for cash, but we all know that the reality is that we have to finance. The point that I am trying to drive home is not using refinance money for other things. It's great to refinance and get a better rate, but do not take that money and buy things or have the kitchen redone. Remember, your house is not a piggy bank to borrow money from.

One of the worst justifications is that the increase in the value of the house is going to offset the bigger debt that you have acquired. Maybe there are cases where this is true, but in general this is a bad idea. Remodeling doesn't always dictate a higher selling price, the market does. If you want to redo your kitchen, use your remodeling kitchen savings account, or dividends from your stock investments.

CARS

People love their cars, especially here in L.A. I don't know how many crew people I have seen get on a show and go out and finance a new car. The real challenge with purchasing cars is that we buy with our emotion more than we buy with our logic. We want that new car smell and the talking navigation. Don't get me wrong; I love all those things as much as the next person but is it really worth getting into debt and having to go to work every day for your material things?

The problem is that a majority of crew members purchase cars to get the lowest monthly payment, and that usually means a longer term on the loan. With no down payment, this means that you will most likely be paying more than the car is worth in the end. Instead the price you pay for the car should be the main concern. If a rebate is offered take the rebate and a short loan payoff.

ZERO PERCENT "0%"

If you opt in for a zero percent interest rate be wary. Usually this means that no rebate is offered and you could be paying close if not the full sticker price, leading you to pay more than what the car is worth over time. Also with 0% interest you must read the contract very carefully before entering into the agreement. Many 0% contracts state that if you are late with just one payment, your rate will increase and you could be locked into a high interest loan, plus liable for retroactive interest from the start of the loan.

A friend once proudly told me that he had a 0% interest free loan. He claimed that the dealer who he bought his previous car from called him and told him that he could trade in his old car, for a new one with this magical 0% interest. This might be ok is some circumstances, but not in his. Here is why: His current car was in great working condition and he only had 3 years until it would be paid off. Assuming his payments were $500 a month then he would have a remaining balance of $18,000. (In this example we will assume that maintenance was included in the car loan.)

Now let's look at the purchase of a new car with 0% down. The problem with buying a new car (0% or with an interest rate) is that it depreciates at a faster rate than a used car. As a general rule, new cars depreciate 15 to 20% as soon as you drive it off the lot. It then continues to depreciate at a rate of 7% to12% of the previous year for the life of the car.

Here we can see the difference in the loss of money if a person were to buy a new car or keep his current car after three years of ownership.

New Car Cost	$30,000		
	Depreciation	Loss in value	Car value
Drive of the lot	20%	$6,000	$24,000
1st year of ownership	12%	$2,880	$21,120
2nd year of ownership	12%	$2,534	$18,586
3rd year of ownership	12%	$2,230	$16,355
Total Loss		**$13,645**	

Current Car Value	$18,000		
	Depreciation	Loss in value	Car value
3rd year of ownership	12%	$2,160	$15,840
4th year of ownership	12%	$1,901	$13,939
5th year of ownership	12%	$1,673	$12,266
Total Loss		**$5,734**	

As you can see in the table, if you were to purchase a new car, you would have lost a lot more money over the next three years than if you held onto your current car.

Make sure you understand the amount of loss you will incur when purchasing a new car. Calculate your numbers and get the best deal for your financial situation.

LEASING A CAR

If you lease a car, there are also a group of other fees to take into account such as going over certain a mileage, or the "rent charge," which is the amount charged in addition to any depreciation and amortization, plus there is a purchase option fee that you have to pay at the end of the lease in order to buy the car you have had for the last four or five years. You also have to take maintenance costs into account over everything else.

USED CARS

Remember earlier I referenced the book *The Millionaire Next Door* by Stanley and Danko? It states that 37% of millionaires purchase their cars used. If we want to become something, we must model it. This might be a good place to start. Find a nice reliable used car while you save to buy the car you want with cash.

In Dave Ramsey's book *The Total Money Make Over,* he details a system where you purchase an affordable used car, and continue to save the amount you believe a new car payment would be. At the end of the year, you sell the used car you purchased, take the money you saved and buy a better-used car. You continue to do this until you can afford a brand new car.

Here is an example:

Purchase used car for:	$7,000
Save each month:	$500
End of the year sell car for:	$6,000
Add savings from the year:	($500 x 12) $6,000
Purchase new car for:	$12,000
Save each month:	$500
And so on …	

It will take you a while to have enough to pay for a $30,000 car, but you will be able to pay cash for a $30,000 new car and have no debt in just a few years. Not a bad deal.

TAX RETURNS

Then you get that tax return take 10% of the return and give it to yourself. Then take another 10% to spend on something to enjoy life; a good dinner, or maybe a new coat. You worked hard for that money, have some fun.

Then take the remaining 80% and if you are in debt pay it towards your debt. This includes your mortgage. Just one extra mortgage payment can save you more than you think. Let's suppose that you have a $450,000 mortgage with a 4% interest rate on a 30 year loan. Let's take a look at what happens when you make just one extra payment of $500.

	No Extra Payment	Extra Payment of $500	Savings
Monthly Payment	$2,148.37	$2,648.37	
Time of Loan	30 Years	29 years	1 year
Interest Paid	$323,412.78	$311,277.82	$12,134.96

Holy savings Batman!

You saved $12,134.96 and you will pay off your debt one year earlier. You have to make sure that you tell your mortgage company that you want the extra payment applied to the principle.

If you are not in debt, congratulate yourself for being a rock star. Then invest the money in stocks and watch it make you more money over time. That same $500 invested for 15 years with an annual return of 8% will give you approximately $1,586. Not a bad way to more than double your money.

MEANING

As crew members we make a lot of money. The problem is that for a lot of us, we have to continue to make a lot of money for all the stuff that we buy. It's a vicious circle that does not make you happy. It just provides temporary fulfillment until you find the next thing to buy. Don't get me wrong, it is nice to have cool stuff, but do not let your stuff define you. Make it your goal to have an enjoyable balanced life. Make sure you have savings, vacations, a few things, family and friends. Break the cycle of what society deems you should have. If you have stuff and it works then keep it. There is no need to run out and buy the latest of everything, especially at the long-term cost of depreciation. Most everything you buy loses value. Have you ever sold a couch for more than you bought it?

Most people purchase things without thinking about the long-term cost. It is important to ask yourself a few questions when purchasing things. Do I really need it? **Most of the time it is not the things that we want, but the feeling that it gives us**. It is important not to lie to yourself. Are you buying something because you want it, or are you trying to gain something else? This can be especially true when it comes to cars. A lot of crew members take on huge car payments for impractical cars that they think will impress their peers. Do not be that person! Buy things and enjoy life, just don't get caught up. In the end you have to do what is financially smart for you and your family.

EXPLANATION

WHICH TYPE OF MONEY PERSON ARE YOU?

In the industry, crew members have different ways in which they react to money. Time to figure out which type sounds most like you ...

The Savers –

These are crew members that are very frugal and save every bit of money. This is good; however there can be extreme savers who sacrifice the enjoyments of life in order to save more money. This reminds me of an old tale about a man who buries his gold in the back yard. Every day for years, he goes to the spot it's buried and just looks at the spot. One day he arrives to see that the hole is dug up and his gold is gone. His neighbor hears his desperate cries and runs over to see what is wrong. After the man with the missing gold calms down, the neighbor tells the man "just fill the hole and continue to visit it every day, as it will be the same, since your gold is never used."

The Worriers –

These are crew members that are constantly worried about money, and act as if they will never have enough. No matter

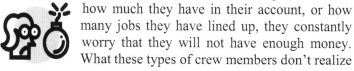

how much they have in their account, or how many jobs they have lined up, they constantly worry that they will not have enough money. What these types of crew members don't realize is that worrying about money or any problem doesn't do anything. Worrying never has changed a circumstance. It either is or isn't going to happen. The best thing is to properly prepare. In the case of money, just understand that there is plenty of work for everybody, and it always works out.

The Avoiders –

These individuals do not want to look at their finances. Their heart races and little beads of sweat forms on their foreheads when the subject of money is brought up. While doing researching for this book, I came across a lot of crew members that just didn't want to know what their finances looked like. They had a general idea, but to sit down and actually look at a simple balance sheet that showed their monthly income and their monthly expense, terrified them. I know that it can be scary. I was there once. I remember taking money out of the ATM and not wanting to look at the balance, or even worse walking up to the ATM not sure if the card was even going to work because of the lack of funds. (I was an avoider for many years of my life, but through steps, similar to the ones laid out in this book, I was able to change my feelings and thoughts towards money, and take control of my finances.)

The Spenders –

These crew members work hard, and make a lot of money, but they always seem to need something more. They love to justify their purchased with, "I got a great deal on it" or "It was on sale," or my personal favorite, "I needed it." Compulsive spenders lie about how much money they spend, and what they spend money on. Spenders are constantly justifying their spending and cannot keep a large sum of money long before they spend it. I also fell into this category for many years. Don't get me wrong; in life we do need stuff. I am talking about the unnecessary items or purchases such as a new couch, when your current one is only a year old.

ACTION

Take a minute and decide which category or categories you fall into.

The Saver
The Worrier
The Avoider
The Spender

INTERESTING FACT

What you measure grows. There is a unique phenomenon when it comes to money. It turns out that when you start to track your spending and your savings, your money starts to grow. All of a sudden you have more money in your accounts than you had before.

SUMMARY

You trade your time for money, and you trade your money for things. Make sure that a when you make this trade, the time of your life that you gave up, is worth the material things. Be aware of your core reasons for buying. Don't blindly buy.

 What To Do ...

1. Be conscious of your spending, and aware that most of the time the item is not needed.

RESOURCES

Visit *wwww.TheWealthyCrewMember.com* to download your *Spending Worksheet* and get yourself on the road to becoming a wealthy crew member.

TIME FOR A DRINK!

Popular in the 1940s, and first served at the Cock 'n Bull tavern in Hollywood, this drink became very popular with the movie crowd.

THE MOSCOW MULE

Ingredients:

- ½ a lime
- Ice
- 2 onces vodka
- 4 to 6 ounces chilled ginger beer

Preparation:

Squeeze lime into a Collins glass (or copper mug, if you've got one) and drop in the spent lime shell. Fill glass with ice and add vodka; top with chilled ginger beer to taste.

Cheers!

PART III

Sprinklers

Once the labor of putting in sprinklers is done, a timer automates when and where the sprinklers will work. The sprinklers continually work for you with little effort on your part. The small amount of work in the beginning will lead to a greener future.

HAVE YOUR MONEY WORK FOR YOU

L et your money work for you! It is not only important that you keep a portion of what you make, but that you also invest that portion. Allow your money the option to compound and make you more money whenever possible. It is important to create a mindset that your money is a willing servant to help you.

UNDERSTANDING

> "The safe way to double your money is to fold it over once and put it in your pocket."
>
> *- Anonymous*

A Tale of Two Crew Members

Paul and Mike are both crew members who work in the entertainment industry and live in the same neighborhood. They coincidentally both got hired on the same feature. Mike has a brand new car he drives, but also has an RV, and a boat in his driveway. Paul has one car that he uses. It is old, but the body is clean and it runs well.

Most of what Paul's owns is old, and outdated. However, Mike always has the latest stuff for work and home. The neighbors watch Paul and Mike and talk about Mike's success. They whisper among themselves that Paul must not make very much money in the industry. After all, his house has not been updated; he mows his lawn with a push mower and does all the repairs to his house himself. It seems like Mike's family has it much better. They own all the "toys" and are remodeling their kitchen after just having a new deck put in.

On Thursday Paul and Mike both head to the credit union and deposit their checks. This happens for the next 4 months of the show. At the beginning of each month Mike goes online and visits his new car financer's website, the RV financier's website, and the boat company's financier's website to pay them. He then pays his mortgage, which he refinanced and took money out to remodel the kitchen. When he finally logs off, the account that he deposited all those checks into over the last few weeks is pretty low. He uses the remainder to give to his wife to buy groceries. She spends most of her time looking for deals in the supermarket flyers.

At the beginning of the month Paul also visits the car dealer website, an RV website, and a boat website. However, after Paul logs off, his bank account that he deposited his check in is bigger. How is this? Well, Paul lives below his means. His needs are simple and he has a surplus of money each month.

Paul noticed that Mike always bought the most popular things. He decided to take his money and invest in those companies. In return he receives dividends on his stock investments every month that are deposited directly into his account.

Mike, the one who appears to be doing better, has to pay back all the money that he has borrowed, while his stuff is depreciating in value. He purchased his newest car with no money down, and then he took more loans out for the RV and the boat. He buys most of the things he "really needs" and puts it on his credit card that has a low interest rate, but he never is able to pay it all off. When he makes purchases with the credit card that has a high balance, he justifies it with the fact that he is gaining airline miles. Unfortunately, Mike will never be able to use them before they expire because he can never afford to take time off of work to use them. All of Mike's money was tied up in paying for his things.

Paul has plenty of money for him and his family. Each month he and his wife pay all their fixed expenses and then discuss the needs for the family. They decide what they really need; clothes for the kids, soccer lessons, and other necessities. Paul and his wife put money in separate accounts so that they can budget accordingly. Paul then researches some potential investment options and invests a percentage of his money after his expenses are paid. He makes sure that he doesn't just put his money in some investments and wait, but that he spends a few hours a month tracking his investments. Indeed a second job, but worth the security of knowing he can choose the jobs he takes and is able to take time off when he wants. After just a few years Paul and his wife are able to also buy a new car and have their kitchen remodeled, but without incurring any debt.

Mike on the other hand, sinks deeper and deeper in debt. Mike's family is use to the latest and newest stuff, always wanting more. His kids grow tired of their video games and want new things they see on TV. At night, Mike worries that his show is about to end and he hasn't lined up work. He thinks to him, "One of these days, I'm going to get ahead." Then his thoughts turn to a deal he saw on the latest super blender, as he drifts off to sleep.

"If money management isn't something you enjoy, consider my perspective. I look at managing my money as if it were a part-time job. The time you spend monitoring your finances will pay off. You can make real money by cutting expenses and earning more interest on savings and investments. I'd challenge you to find a part-time job where you could potentially earn as much money for just an hour or two of your time."

- *Laura D. Adams*

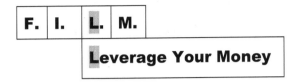

F.	I.	L.	M.

Leverage Your Money

MEANING

It doesn't matter how much money you make. What matters is how much you make work for you. There is only one real way to find security in the freelance business of the Film Industry; spend less than you make, invest, and save. It's as simple as that.

Why Is Investing So Important?

In one word I can tell you why it is important to invest... inflation. Inflation is the rate at which prices for goods and services raise and the value of the dollar falls. For example, if the price of a six pack of beer costs $8 and the inflation rate is around 3%, then that 6 pack will cost you $8.24 after inflation. Not a big difference, but over time inflation can hurt you financially. What you could purchase for $5.00 in 1995 is not the same as what you can purchase in 2013, and this is due to inflation. Can you see how this is a problem and how your purchasing power is diminished? This is why it is important that you take the money that you earn and invest it in order to beat inflation.

If you have money in a regular savings account at your bank, the chances are that the interest paid to you is not enough to cover the difference in the inflation rise. This means that your money is actually weakening and decreasing your purchasing power. This implies that the next year an item you want will cost more, but you won't have enough money. Your money will not grow fast enough to keep up with the rising prices. It is through investing you beat the rise in inflation and your hard earned dollars stay as valuable.

I love Compound Interest like a fat kid loves cake!

One of the greatest wonders in the world is compound interest. This is because your initial investment will continue to grow because of reinvested interest earnings. The money feeds on itself and grows. You put money in an account and interest is applied to that account every year. So the next year, you gain interest not only on your initial invested amount, but on the interest that amount has made as well. Put your money in and let it grow. Of course a high interest rate is preferred and the earlier you start saving the more growth your initial investment will experience.

If you put $100 away each month for 20 years, you will have saved $24,000. However, once you add compound interest over the 20 years, and assume your average rate of return is 8%; your $24,000 investment will be worth approximately $59,300. Imagine if you saved $1,000 a month... ok I'll tell you, it would be almost $594,000 in just $20 years.

Now take a look at this compound interest chart showing what your return would be if you were to invest only $1,000 at an 8% annual rate of return over a period of 5 to 25 years.

83

Amount Invested:	$1,000	
Rate of Return:	8%	
Years Invested	Future Amount	Profit
5	$1,469	$469
10	$2,159	$1,159
20	$4,661	$3,661
25	$6,849	$5,849

I know what you are thinking…where the heck am I going to get an 8% return on my money? Well, this is where the importance of diversifying your investments comes into play. I will discuss diversification and your investment options in a later section to follow. Plus it is also important to point out that the S&P 500, which is a market index consisting of the largest companies in America, and considered the most accurate measure of the stock market, has averaged an 11.68% rate of return between 1926 and 2012. A much better return than those Taco Bell collector cups that you bought in the early 90's!

EXPLANATION

INVESTING TIPS FOR CREW MEMBERS

We all know that we should invest our money. Before we begin, let's take a quick quiz to find out how much financial knowledge you have. The answers can be found at the end of the book. Remember, this quiz is just to get you in the right mindset. It doesn't matter how you do.

1 Suppose you have $1,000 in a savings account earning 7% percent (compound) interest a year. In five years how much would you have?

A. More than $1,350
B. Exactly $1,350
C. Less than $1,350

2 Let us suppose one of your M.A.D. accounts named "new refrigerator" is gaining an interest rate of 5 % a year. If inflation were 6 % a year, at the end of the year would the money in the account be able to purchase more or less than it does today.

A. More
B. Less

3 The total interest on a 15 year mortgage will be less and will have higher monthly payments than if you were to take on a 30 year mortgage.

A. True
B. False

4 When interest rates rise, bond prices fall.

A. True
B. False
C. There is no relationship to bond price and interest rates.

5 Stocks are safer than mutual funds, and junk bonds.

A. True
B. False

ACTION

How can I figure out how long it will take to double my money? (The Rule of 72)

The rule of 72 is a simple math equation that investors use to estimate length of double return. You can use it to find out the number of years it will take to double your money. It is simple! All you have to do is divide 72 by the expected rate of return, and it will give you the number of years it will take for your money to double. So for example, if you invested a sum of money at a 12% return rate, it will take you six years (72/12 = 6) to double your money. Math is cool!

INVESTING

In order to invest you must be aware of what is going on in the market. In the next two weeks, spend at least 15 minutes a day reading investment blogs. A great way to make sure you do this is to change your internet home page to a financial page. This way, every time you log into the computer you are reminded of it, and can spend a few minutes reading about what the market is doing.

You can also visit virtual trading websites like *www.howthemarketworks.com* to practice trading. I like this website because they use real time stock prices. This will help you get used to putting your money in the market.

If you chose to hire a financial adviser, make sure that they are **fee only advisors** and not fee based advisors. Fee only advisors make their commission based on what you purchase and do not sell products such as mutual funds and annuities. If you want mutual funds or annuities they will recommend where to purchase them. The Fee based financial advisors sell products and may not have your best interest at hand.

Discount brokers charge a commission to purchase your investments for you, but do not give you any advice. If you do your own research, I would suggest using an online discount brokerage since they usually charge the lowest commission.

DIVERSIFYING

Diversifying simply means to invest through different channels. Mutual funds, stocks, bonds, your grandma's tea cozy Etsy business etc... This way your risk is spread out. You won't lose all your money if one investment or sector tanks.

The idea behind diversifying is that if your money is in not just one, but many different kinds of investments, then on average you will make more money, and it will be less risky than if you just had one investment. I cannot stress how important a diversified portfolio is. Don't put all your eggs in one basket! The only exception to this is that if you are close to retirement, you should be more conservative with your investments. Financial advisers usually recommend that the closer you are to retirement, the more heavily you should be invested in low risk investments such as bonds. If you are more than 20 years from retirement then financial advisers suggest putting around 70% in stocks and 30% into bonds. You can be a bit more aggressive in the stock market at this point, as you have more time to recover from any market losses.

DOLLAR COST AVERAGING (DCA)

DCA is the system of investing a fix amount regardless of the market price for a fixed amount of time. Over time you will make more money than if you had invested a lump sum. For example you have $100 every month taken out to buy Apple stock regardless of the price of the stock, you would make more money in the long run than if you just purchased Apple stock every time it was a good share price. The Vanguard Group compared investing a lump sum of $1 million to investing it dollar-cost averaging. The result was that the lump sum investors lost value around 22% of the time, while DCA investors incurred a loss of only 18% on average.

INVESTMENT VEHICLES

Certificate of Deposit - CDs

If you are looking for a safe investment, then CDs are for you. A CD is a certificate of deposit. Basically you agree to loan the bank a certain amount of money for a fixed period of time, and when that time period is over, the bank returns your initial investment plus the agreed upon interest rate. The more money you put in, the higher the return you are going to get. Note that when you purchase a CD, your money is locked in, and if you need to withdraw it prior to the maturity date, you will pay an early withdrawal penalty. Some banks do offer liquid CDs, which allow you to take your money out before the agreed upon time and not be penalized. Many online banks offer a higher rate on CDs as compared to brick and mortar banks. Compare rates before deciding on which bank to use. You might want to consider a broker, because they work for firms that buy large CDs and break them down and sell them at smaller amounts. Make sure that you reinvest your interest! Unfortunately today the rates on CDs are relatively low, so your return will be significantly lower than when investing in other investment assets, but this offers a low risk guaranteed return.

Stocks

There are two kinds of stocks: Income/Value stocks that typically pay out their profits to their investors via dividends, and Growth stocks that are shares in companies that reinvest their profits into the company to promote growth. Stocks prices will go up as the company becomes more profitable. Penny stocks usually sell for less than $5, while some set the cut off at $3.00 or lower. Stocks are considered to be a more risky investment, and it is recommended for someone who is willing to actively review and manage their portfolio. Make sure you research performance trends before purchasing stocks.

Mutual Funds

Mutual funds are made up of multiple investments. The fund manager will buy and sell the best securities for growth of the mutual fund. There are different types of funds that you can choose from depending on your investment strategy. When you buy into in a mutual fund you are investing into a pool of money, from several investors such as yourself, that is managed by a professional fund manager. His or her job is to buy and sell individual assets owed by the fund to generate increased returns. The benefit of investing in a mutual fund is that it allows for more diversification. However, there is generally a fee associated with buying into a mutual fund, so do your homework on historical fund performance and fees before you invest.

89

Index Funds

Index funds are basically mutual funds, but are passively managed. The fund matches the stock market exactly. They are usually tied to an index; the most popular being the S&P 500 (Standard and Poor's Index). Fees associated with index funds are generally lower than other mutual funds. You will do as well as the stock market does, but never beat the market. Research shows that when investing over a longer period of time, index funds tend to outperform mutual funds.

Bonds

Bonds are investments that are loans to a corporation or government. When you purchase a bond it is only for a certain amount of time and pays you a fixed interest rate. It's basically an IOU. Agencies issue bonds in order to fund projects. These are usually government-backed investments, so they are low risk investments; and therefore generally generate lower returns.

The best thing to do is diversify and buy a little bit of everything. Dedicate percentages to invest amongst the various investing vehicles based on how risky you want to be, and by your age.

INTERESTING FACT

The right side of your brain is responsible for emotional responses. According to research this side of the brain often overrides the left or logical side of the brain when it comes to investing. This is why we may invest on a gut feeling instead relying on logic. So the goal is to get your left-brain to pay attention.

SUMMARY

Remember it is ok to invest just a $100. The amount of money doesn't matter. Most people think that they need a ton of money to invest. Although it is true that some investments have limits, there are others that don't. Find investments that suit your budget and jump in. You will be happy you did.

What To Do ...

1. Spend at least 15 minutes a day reading investment blogs.
2. Decide where you are going to put your money.
3. Start investing, even if it's only a small amount.

RESOURCES

- Visit *www.treasurydirect.gov* where you can find a list of government bonds, including the popular ibond.

- For online trading and investing.
  www.Schwab.com
  www.Vanguard.com
  www.TDAmeritrade.com
  www.ETrade.com
  www.Scotttrade.com

AUTOMATE YOUR LIFE

*T*he trouble with managing money can often be traced to the inability of the individual to keep focused on their finances. By having a system that is fully automated, the system of wealth is allowed to happen without interference. Allow automation to lead you to becoming a wealthy crew member.

UNDERSTANDING

F.	I.	L.	M.

Manage Your System

It is important to set up a system, but more importantly it is important to set up an automatic system. This is where your system is not dependent on you, but is happening even when you don't have time to pay attention to it.

MEANING

If you have an automatic system in place, then it's as if you are automating your habit. You can save and invest by having the money taken out automatically. This works because before you have time to spend the money for something else, the money is gone and used for its intended purpose.

Automation is a great way to force you to be a wealthy crew member. Now that you have a better understanding of your expenses, your monthly or average income, and are *M.A.D. F.I.T*, it is time to automate. The key to successful money management is automation. Over a decade ago when I first started the M.A.D. system, there wasn't the automation that there is today. Today you can automate your life, and that is what we are going to do.

The best way to do this is to automate your savings contributions, and have money automatically sent to your retirement brokerage account and to your savings account.

ACTION

Paychecks

If you don't see the money going into your account, then you are less likely to spend it. Most payroll companies have automatic deposit. It's free to sign up, and your checks will be automatically deposited into your bank of choice.

Once you figure out the percentages that you want to contribute to each of your accounts, based on the M.A.D. system, you can have that amount automatically transferred to each account. This is especially valuable for your retirement account.

I would recommend that you only get a debit card for the *basic needs account*, *fun account*, and joint accounts. With savings accounts limit your accessibility and do not get a debit card. Hopefully the fact that you need to go into the bank to withdraw your money will help you save.

Bills

If you have ever been late on a bill, then automation is going to save you. In fact every bill should be automated through your bank. This will prevent any late fees from ever occurring, and it is one less hassle in your life. One of the best things is to have all your bills due on the same date preferably in the beginning of the month. You can call most companies including credit card companies and chose the date on which you are billed.

If the bill is consistent like rent or a mortgage, then you can fully automate and have your bank pay the service every month. If the bill varies, then you can go onto your banks website and manually enter the amounts to be paid each month. You should develop the habit of paying bills once a month on the same day. If an unexpected bill arrives, make it a habit to pay it right away. Living in Los Angeles, I occasionally get parking tickets. After the cursing, I pay it that same day and am done with it. Most people put off paying tickets, as if waiting will make the fine go away. Admit you messed up, pay it right away, and move on.

The best way to automate bills is to sign up to pay all your bills through your bank instead of signing up for individual company auto pay services. The reason being is that you want to give as few people access to your account as possible. Also if you are double billed, it will be a far longer process to correct the mistake than if your bank makes one on their end. This helps you also if you get a new debit or credit card and you have auto bill set up through an individual company, if you lose your card, or a card is reissued you will have to contact all the companies to let them know. If you forget you could be missing payments and not know of it. This could lead to a ding on your credit report. So, keep the control and set up automation through your banks. Even if you automate your payments, it still is important to look over your statements to make sure that the appropriate charges are being made.

You may also chose to pay all your bills on a credit card that has no annual fee and offers you airline miles. Just make sure that you pay your credit card every month. If you have a bad habit of being late and accruing interest, then do not use credit cards.

To monitor your bills, I highly recommend *Mint.com*. It is a free system that helps you to keep track of your spending and tracks your net worth. You can use it to help budget, and set goals. For example you can set a spending budget for groceries at $1,000 and every time you spend it will tell you how much you have left. This omits blind spending. When it comes to spending the wealthy crew member knows how much to spend.

INTERESTING FACT

It costs approximately 6.4 cents per note to produce U.S. currency.

SUMMARY

The key to any efficient system can be linked to automation. When you automate you are guaranteed that the system in place will work.

What To Do ...

1. Set up your bills to be automatically paid from your bank accounts.

2. Set up a system of saving where your money is automatically deducted from you paychecks and transferred to an interest bearing account.

RESOURCE

- ING *(www.ing.com)* is an online FDIC insured bank and offers higher interest rates than a brick and mortar bank.
- First Internet Bank *(www.Firstib.com)* is FDIC insured and offers higher interest rates than brick and mortar banks.
- First Entertainment Credit Union (www.Firstent.org) is the credit union for members of the film industry.
- Mint *(www.Mint.com)* offers a free tool to organize and categorize your spending.

INVEST FOR THE FUTURE

*I*n order to enjoy things in the future you must plan for them now. Do not be fooled into thinking that things will just work out. It is through conscious decisions made with your money that you will be able to live the life that you desire when you retire.

UNDERSTANDING

> *"You can be young without money, but you can't be old without it."*
>
> **– Tennessee Williams**

By now hopefully you have learned something about money management. The following section is one of the most important chapters in this book. I have invested hours researching books, talking with financial advisors, and visiting our union and motion picture industry pension and health plan office in order to make this as simple and understandable as possible. The next chapter lays out a clear step by step process that will allow you to determine your current and future retirement needs so that you may create a plan for a comfortable life while in retirement. Although it is simplified, it still may be a little challenging. Don't get discouraged. Take it step by step. Good luck.

In 2012, The International Alliance of Theatrical Stage Employees, which represents 38,000 of us behind-the-scenes workers in the film and television industries, ratified a three-year contract with Hollywood producers. Our locals (15 to be exact) who represent IATSE members agreed to a 2% annual wage increase over a period of three years.

The average pay increase from the last 20 years has been around 3%. The problem is that the Bureau of Labor Statistics averages inflation rates around 3.4%. That is a not enough to keep up with inflation. This means that the cost of that $500 TV you are going to buy goes up 3.4%, but your money earned is going to be worth 0.4% less.

MEANING

Just like you plan for your vacations, and buying those flat screen TV's, you must plan for your retirement.

Save as much as you can for retirement! I cannot reiterate this enough. **Just because you work a lot of years does not mean that you will be taken care of or have enough for your retirement.** You have to be proactive. It is important that you have additional money saved because your pension and Social Security is supplemental income and most likely won't be enough to live on. You will still need more money to live a decent lifestyle.

The good news is that you have made the amazing decision to buy this book, and with some planning and effort I am going to help get you on the path to making sure that you are well prepared for retirement, and that you will not reach retirement and suddenly realize that you don't have enough to live on so you are forced to apply for government assistance, and eat cat food while you wait on your checks.

EXPLANATION

How much do I need for retirement? How much do I need to save now?

Chances are you don't really know how much you need for retirement, because you just haven't given it much thought, or you think that your pension will be enough for you to live on. Well instead of guessing let's take a minute here and get a really good estimate of how much you are going to need, and how much you need to save in order to get to your retirement goals.

In order to find out how much you will have for retirement, what you have to do is figure out how much money you are going to have in the future. This is done in a few simple steps.

First by adding an average percentage of pay increase (IATSE members have averaged 3% over the last 20 years) to the average amount of money you make every year, then that number is multiplied by the amount of working years until you retire. Next you will take your pension and Social Security and find out how much it will be worth in the future. Finally you will add your Individual account retirement plan and any other investments that you currently have and work out how much they will be worth in the future.

CALCULATING HOW MUCH YOU NEED FOR RETIREMENT

1. *80% of your current income multiplied by the inflation factor.*
2. *Subtract your Social Security, Pension, IRA, and any other future income. Adjust for inflation.*
3. *Determine how much money needs to be saved each month till retirement.*

So let's look at an example; then you can work out what you will need.

Determining amount needed to live when retired

Most financial advisers recommend that you will need around 80% of your current income to live on after retirement. This is because most likely your expenses will be reduced by 20% (e.g. Mortgage, kids,) when retired. In our example crew member Jack is 42 years old and is currently making $100,000 a year. So Jack will need $80,000 a year ($100,000 x 80% = $80,000) to live on in retirement.

Now let's suppose that Jack plans to retire in 25 years, and the rate of inflation is 4% annually. In order to adjust for this inflation, we can use the *Inflation Factor Chart (4% Annual Inflation)* on the next page. Since Jack will retire in 25 years, we can use a factor of 2.67. By multiplying $80,000 by the 2.67 factor ($80,000 x 2.67), we can determine that he will need about $213,600 a year to live while in retirement.

Question: What the hell is an inflation factor?
Answer: It helps simplify the calculations to determine future value of money.

Inflation Factor Chart (4% Annual Inflation)

# of years until retirement	Inflation Factor
30	3.24
25	2.67
20	2.19
15	1.80
10	1.48

Amount needed to live when Jack is retired: $213,600

The next step is to determine how much Jack can expect to receive from his Social Security and pension plan. We will then subtract this amount from what we determined Jack will need to live upon retirement.

Determining Social Security Payouts

In this example, if Jack were to retire at 67 years old, he would receive $2,496 a month from Social Security. So each year, Jack will receive $29,952 ($2,496 x 12 months) from social security.

If you start your benefits:	And you earn an average of:	Your benefits will be about:
At full retirement (age 67)	$100,000 a year (from now until full retirement)	$2,496 a month
At age 70	$100,000 a year (from now until age 70)	$3,122 a month
At age 62	$100,000 a year (from now until age 62)	$1,705 a month

Let's adjust Jack's Social Security for inflation.

To determine what Jack's money will be worth in terms of future dollars, we need to adjust for inflation. We'll apply a 4% inflation rate for this example, and therefore use a factor of 2.67 (refer to *Inflation Factor Chart*) since he will retire in 25 years. So Jack's annual social security payout of $29,952 (calculated above) will be worth $79,972 ($29,952 x 2.67) a year in future dollars after adjusting for inflation.

Jack's Social Security future yearly payout: $79,972

Determining Pension Payouts

Jack will receive an annual pension of $12,000 a year for all his years of hard work on set.

Let's adjust Jack's Pension for inflation.

Just like we adjusted Jack's social security payout to determine its value in 25 years, adjusted for 4% inflation, we need calculate what Jack's pension will be in future dollars. When Jack retires, each year, his annual $12,000 payout will be worth $32,040 ($12,000 x 2.67) a year in future dollars.

Pension future yearly payout: $32,040

Determining the gap between what is needed versus what is received when retired

Remember above we found out that Jack will need $213,600 (adjusted for inflation) each year he is retired? Now we are going to subtract the money he will receive from social security and his pension from that amount needed for retirement to determine how much he still needs.

(a)	Money needed *(annual)* =	**$213,600**
(b)	**Retirement Payouts** *(annual)*	
	Social Security *(annual)* =	$79,972
	Pension *(annual)* =	$32,040
	Society Security + Pension =	**$112,012**
	Money still needed (a – b) =	**$101,588**

Jack is short by **$101,588** (adjusted for inflation) for his retirement **each year**.

We will assume that Jack will retire at 67 and live until 86. That is 19 years of retirement for Jack until he goes to that big movie set in the sky. In order for us to calculate how much money Jack will still need in total during his retired life, we have to multiply $101,588 by 19 years, which is **$1,930,172** (adjusted for inflation).

This shows us that in order for Jack to retire and live just below his current lifestyle, he will need to save $1,930,172 more in future dollars.

Total amount still needed to be saved: $1,930,172

Determining how much money needs to be saved each month till retirement

Jack has a retirement account through the Motion Picture Health Plan worth $80,000. The average return on this Individual Account Plan (IAP) is 8%. Now we will leverage the factor chart below to determine what $80,000 will be worth in 25 years. We can use the 6.85 as our factor to determine what the account will be worth in 25 years at an 8% rate of return. So in total, Jack's IAP account will be worth $548,000 ($80,000 x 6.85) when he retires.

		Rate				
		4%	5%	8%	10%	12%
	10	1.48	1.63	2.16	2.59	3.11
Years	15	1.8	2.08	3.17	4.18	5.47
	20	2.19	2.65	4.66	6.73	9.65
	25	2.67	3.39	6.85	10.82	17.00

Earlier we calculated that Jack still needs $1,930,172 over and above his social security and pension payouts. We just determined that in 25 years his IAP balance will be around **$548,000**. We can now subtract this from how much he needs.

Money still needed post S.S & Pension	$1,930,172
IAP Balance in 25 years @ 8% rate of return	- $548,000
Total Money still needed to be saved	**= $1,382,172**

As shown above, Jack will need to save an additional $1,382,172 in total to live at his comfort level when retired. Now we can take how much he needs and divide it by how many years he has until he retires. Since Jack will retire in 25 years, he will need to save **$55,287** ($1,382,172 / 25) each year.

Finally in order for us to determine how much Jack needs to save per month each year till retirement, we can divide the amount he needs to save annual by twelve. This tells us that Jack will need to save **$4,607** a month in order to reach his retirement goals.

Monthly savings determined: $4,607

ACTION

I understand if keeping up with Jack's retirement example may have been a bit overwhelming, so let's break it down into simple steps such that you can figure out what you will need for your retirement.

1 *Take your current annual income and multiply it by 80%.*

2 *Multiply Step 1 by an inflation factor from chart below.*

Current income adjusted for future inflation.

Inflation Factor Chart

# of years until retirement	Avg. rate of inflation
30	3.24
25	2.67
20	2.19
15	1.80
10	1.48

3 *Add up your Social Security and Pension payouts that you will receive each year.*

*Visit the Social Security website to determine your payout.
http://www.ssa.gov/retire2/AnypiaApplet.html

108

4 *Multiply Step 3 by an inflation factor.*

> ** Multiply by same inflation factor that you used from the chart above.*

5 *Subtract Step 4 from Step 2.*

> *Amount Needed*

6 *Now multiply by Step 5 by number of years of retirement.*

Ok, now take a deep breath. Remember this is only an estimate, but the fact is that you have to start investing some money now so that you can get a high return. As I mentioned earlier the Standards and Poor's Index fund has had an average return of 12%. So that is good news!

Now what we are going to do is find out how much you will have to save each month from now on in order to reach your retirement goals.

Now let's see how much you have to save in order to reach your retirement goal ...

How much do I need to start saving every month?

7 *Take your Individual Account Plan (IAP) and any other investments into account that you may have and multiply them by a factor in the chart below.*

			Rate		
		4%	5%	8%	10%	12%
Years	10	1.48	1.63	2.16	2.59	3.11
	15	1.8	2.08	3.17	4.18	5.47
	20	2.19	2.65	4.66	6.73	9.65
	25	2.67	3.39	6.85	10.82	17.00

8 *Take the amount from Step 7 and subtract it from Step 6.*

The difference will give you the amount you need to save each year.

9 *Divide step 8 by the number of years you have until retirement.*

10 *Divide step 9 by 12 months to get the amount you should be putting in savings every month.*

11 *Freak Out!*

You must remember that this is just an estimate of what you may need. Also, you may be able to live on less than 80% of your current income. 80% percentage was used because it is always better to overestimate.

Upon retirement, if you have been paying down your house and if the property has appreciated in value over the years, you may be able to use the equity that you have built up in your home; only if you decide to move into a smaller place, and you haven't borrowed against it already. This is another reason not to use your home equity as a piggy bank, but treat it as savings by never borrowing against it.

I.A.T.S.E. PENSION

I have spent months learning about our IATSE pension so that I may be able to simplify it for you. For a more detailed explanation please visit your union representatives and the Motion Picture Pension plan office to meet with a qualified representative.

Here is how your pension plan works…Once you have worked for 10 years and each of those 10 years you work a minimum of 400 hours each year, you become vested. This means that the money that your employers contribute to your pension and individual retire account cannot be taken from you, even if you leave the industry.

If you have less than 20 years with the union, then you must work at least 400 hours each year in order for your employer to contribute to your pension plans. If you have over 20 years in the industry, you don't need the 400 hours in order receive employer contributions when you work.

For every hour you work, the employer contributes an amount for every hour you work. As of this writing it is $0.03729 for every hour you work, if you have less than 10 years in the industry. After 10 years the producers currently contribute $0.04972 for each hour worked.

INDIVIDUAL RETIREMENT ACCOUNT

Employers also contribute 6% of your rate to your individual account plan. This is the industries version of an IRA with the exception that you cannot contribute to it. It works like this- They take your rate and multiply it by the hours that you work; and then they contribute 6% of that total to your IAP. Your hourly rate is the base and does not change to account for your over time rate.

HEALTH BENEFITS (I.A.T.S.E)

The employer also contributes money to your medical, dental and vision health plans. See the Motion Picture Health office for exact numbers for your job group.

If you have 15 years with the union, 20,000 hours on the job, and have worked no less than 400 hours for three years after the age of 40, then you are eligible for medical coverage when you turn 62. The years do not have to be consecutive. You just have to work 3 additional years and accumulate 400 hours any time after the age of 40. You may even leave this industry and remain eligible for full medical when you turn 62. Not a bad deal!

We are very fortunate to have this health care benefit. I would like to thank the employers, the unions, and the guilds from the 1950's who agreed to establish a pension plan, and an individual account plan (IAP) on our behalf. However, with that being said, most crew members are relying on their pension and IAP to live off of during retirement. This is not the best plan. As shown above when you calculated how much money you need for retirement, your pension and IAP are supplemental income, and most likely will not be enough to maintain a lifestyle at 80% of your current income. This is why you have to invest and save your money.

D.G.A. PENSION

If you are in the DGA (Directors Guild of America) you have a Basic Pension Plan and a Supplemental Pension Plan. Your employer will make pension contributions equal to 5.5% of your gross salary up to a certain cap.

The Basic Plan is based on your total years of service and 3.3% of your earnings are contributed by your employer, up to the allowable amount allowed by the IRS is contributed.

The Supplemental Plan has your employer contributing 2.2% of your first $150,000 earned plus the entire 5.5% of earnings over $150,000 credited to your Individual Account.

You receive 1 credited service month for every $3,000 you make a year with a maximum of 12 Credited service months a year.

For calculating your future supplemental plan money it is safe to use an 8% return.

D.G.A. HEALTH PLAN

Guild membership does not mean that you will have health benefits. The D.G.A qualifies members for health benefits by the amount of income made in a qualified period. There are two plans, one for members who make between $34,100-$105,999 in earnings and a premiere plan for members that make $106,000 or more in earnings

SAVING ON YOUR OWN FOR RETIREMENT

There are a few different retirement account options. Some allow you to invest pre tax dollars and others, post tax money. Let's take a look at the different options.

Roth IRA - Individual Retirement Account

A Roth IRA is an individual retirement account that offers tax-free income upon retirement. It is considered one of the best places to save your money. Every dollar of *post tax money* that you contribute to a Roth IRA is yours, so you can withdraw it at any time after 5 years without having to pay taxes. There is also no early withdrawal fee. However, you are just not allowed to withdraw the earnings on your money before you are 59 ½ years old. The Roth IRA allows for compounded growth and penalty free withdrawal. If you wait until after you are 70 ½ you will be charged a 50% penalty for late withdraw. Single people earning less than $112,000 can contribute the maximum of $5,500. If you are married and your combined annual income is less than $178,000, every year each of you can contribute $5,500.

Traditional IRA- Individual Retirement Account

This has the same contributions limits as the Roth IRA ($5,500) with the exception being that you invest *pretax* money. This means that you contribute money before you are taxed, and when you withdraw the money upon retirement, you will be taxed.

Which type of IRA is better for me?

Each person may have their own reasons for choosing one over the other. If you think that you will be in a higher tax bracket when you retire, then the Roth IRA will be most beneficial to you. If you feel you will be in a lower tax bracket and making less at retirement, then the Traditional IRA is the way to go. The key benefit of the Roth IRA is that though your principle investment has been taxed, all gains made over the years are tax free! The benefit of the Roth IRA is that you are saving more up front. The more you save the better it will be for retirement. It's just the amount of taxes that you have to consider.

What If I Am Non-Union and/or a Production Assistant?

If you are not receiving union benefits, you still need to save for your retirement. Speak with a financial consultant about the best way to start funding your retirement. Mostly likely a Roth IRA will be recommended. There are government restrictions on how much post tax money you can contribute each year. It is important that you maximize the amount of money that you can contribute to your retirement savings every year. Remember compound interest!

INTERESTING FACT

Most people have not adequately saved for their retirement. According to the Employee Benefit Research Institute, 40% of people have less than $25,000 saved for retirement, and almost 50% will run out of money while they are retired.

SUMMARY

It is important that you start to save individually on your own. Down load the worksheets and figure out what you are going to need when you retire. The best time to save for you retirement is yesterday, but the second best time is today!

 What To Do ...

1. Calculate how much you currently have for retirement.
2. Calculate how much you will need for retirement.
3. Set up a plan to achieve your retirement goals

RESOURCES

- Motion Picture Industry Pension and Health plans (*www.MPIPHP.org*)

- IATSE National Benefit funds (www.*IATSEbf.org*)

- Pension and health benefits for DGA members (*www.DGAplans.org*)

- Retirement calculator on *thewealthycrewmember.com*

- Retirement accounts can be opened at …
    www.Fidelity.com
    www.t.roweprice.com
    www.Vanguard.com
    www.Sharebuilder.com
    www.Ameritrade.com

I want to thank you for reading this book and congratulate you on taking the steps to become a wealthy crew member. You now understand that you are in control of your money.

THE BEGINNING...

THE WEALTHY CREW MEMBER'S RULES TO MANAGING MONEY

- HAVE A MONEY MINDSET
- CREATE A CLEAR UNDERSTANDING OF WHERE YOU ARE FINANCAILLY
- IMPLEMENTING A SYSTEM
- KEEP A PORTION OF EVERYTHING YOU MAKE
- CONTROL YOUR SPENDING
- HAVE YOUR MONEY WORK FOR YOU
- INVEST FOR THE FUTURE

Quiz on Page 87   [1.A,   2.B,   3.A,   4.A,   5.B]

Made in the USA
Lexington, KY
15 January 2016